MATH
WORKBOOK

ADDITION & SUBTRACTION

D1709366

ADDITION

1)   25
   + 64
   ....

2)   50
   + 93
   ....

3)   54
   + 17
   ....

4)   61
   + 71
   ....

5)   92
   + 39
   ....

6)   87
   + 71
   ....

7)   70
   + 70
   ....

8)   62
   + 41
   ....

9)   81
   + 55
   ....

10)   51
    + 40
   ....

11)   93
    + 66
   ....

12)   59
    + 28
   ....

13)   90
    + 71
   ....

14)   62
    + 61
   ....

15)   47
    + 84
   ....

16)   16
    + 98
   ....

17)   82
    + 17
   ....

18)   58
    + 99
   ....

19)   85
    + 21
   ....

20)   58
    + 50
   ....

1)　　88
　　+ 16
　　_____

2)　　78
　　+ 21
　　_____

3)　　68
　　+ 90
　　_____

4)　　63
　　+ 30
　　_____

5)　　14
　　+ 50
　　_____

6)　　25
　　+ 71
　　_____

7)　　58
　　+ 82
　　_____

8)　　56
　　+ 18
　　_____

9)　　57
　　+ 14
　　_____

10)　　50
　　+ 70
　　_____

11)　　51
　　+ 10
　　_____

12)　　72
　　+ 54
　　_____

13)　　62
　　+ 79
　　_____

14)　　93
　　+ 38
　　_____

15)　　11
　　+ 51
　　_____

16)　　52
　　+ 25
　　_____

17)　　77
　　+ 45
　　_____

18)　　89
　　+ 70
　　_____

19)　　31
　　+ 40
　　_____

20)　　38
　　+ 41
　　_____

1)   96
    + 35

2)   29
    + 63

3)   97
    + 99

4)   93
    + 23

5)   92
    + 85

6)   85
    + 28

7)   75
    + 20

8)   58
    + 87

9)   16
    + 14

10)   38
    + 85

11)   25
    + 15

12)   16
    + 44

13)   53
    + 59

14)   13
    + 77

15)   88
    + 11

16)   37
    + 96

17)   80
    + 49

18)   44
    + 86

19)   44
    + 41

20)   71
    + 26

1) $\begin{array}{r} 95 \\ + 26 \\ \hline \end{array}$
2) $\begin{array}{r} 34 \\ + 91 \\ \hline \end{array}$
3) $\begin{array}{r} 58 \\ + 88 \\ \hline \end{array}$
4) $\begin{array}{r} 47 \\ + 36 \\ \hline \end{array}$

5) $\begin{array}{r} 75 \\ + 70 \\ \hline \end{array}$
6) $\begin{array}{r} 53 \\ + 74 \\ \hline \end{array}$
7) $\begin{array}{r} 42 \\ + 22 \\ \hline \end{array}$
8) $\begin{array}{r} 13 \\ + 72 \\ \hline \end{array}$

9) $\begin{array}{r} 20 \\ + 69 \\ \hline \end{array}$
10) $\begin{array}{r} 62 \\ + 74 \\ \hline \end{array}$
11) $\begin{array}{r} 42 \\ + 11 \\ \hline \end{array}$
12) $\begin{array}{r} 36 \\ + 29 \\ \hline \end{array}$

13) $\begin{array}{r} 28 \\ + 98 \\ \hline \end{array}$
14) $\begin{array}{r} 11 \\ + 17 \\ \hline \end{array}$
15) $\begin{array}{r} 75 \\ + 52 \\ \hline \end{array}$
16) $\begin{array}{r} 67 \\ + 58 \\ \hline \end{array}$

17) $\begin{array}{r} 32 \\ + 33 \\ \hline \end{array}$
18) $\begin{array}{r} 30 \\ + 66 \\ \hline \end{array}$
19) $\begin{array}{r} 28 \\ + 13 \\ \hline \end{array}$
20) $\begin{array}{r} 87 \\ + 91 \\ \hline \end{array}$

1) $87 + 39$

2) $60 + 33$

3) $13 + 94$

4) $52 + 19$

5) $91 + 46$

6) $54 + 17$

7) $81 + 70$

8) $42 + 51$

9) $75 + 56$

10) $14 + 19$

11) $12 + 27$

12) $47 + 73$

13) $71 + 17$

14) $36 + 86$

15) $27 + 35$

16) $77 + 24$

17) $38 + 38$

18) $14 + 13$

19) $40 + 13$

20) $76 + 31$

1) 68
  + 65

2) 91
  + 66

3) 68
  + 40

4) 78
  + 53

5) 65
  + 39

6) 21
  + 72

7) 78
  + 82

8) 52
  + 24

9) 36
  + 23

10) 26
   + 97

11) 37
   + 73

12) 83
   + 62

13) 16
   + 45

14) 23
   + 72

15) 80
   + 44

16) 21
   + 53

17) 51
   + 80

18) 61
   + 11

19) 95
   + 34

20) 65
   + 27

1)   26
    + 16
    ....

2)   72
    + 31
    ....

3)   28
    + 67
    ....

4)   31
    + 98
    ....

5)   31
    + 51
    ....

6)   28
    + 11
    ....

7)   57
    + 97
    ....

8)   13
    + 12
    ....

9)   77
    + 20
    ....

10)   19
    + 59
    ....

11)   80
    + 95
    ....

12)   59
    + 47
    ....

13)   10
    + 42
    ....

14)   81
    + 86
    ....

15)   21
    + 66
    ....

16)   30
    + 67
    ....

17)   73
    + 42
    ....

18)   11
    + 87
    ....

19)   62
    + 74
    ....

20)   54
    + 86
    ....

1)   85
+ 44

2)   86
+ 65

3)   31
+ 61

4)   37
+ 25

5)   96
+ 25

6)   49
+ 13

7)   65
+ 32

8)   33
+ 25

9)   10
+ 88

10)   33
+ 67

11)   21
+ 19

12)   36
+ 53

13)   49
+ 59

14)   47
+ 72

15)   90
+ 80

16)   41
+ 37

17)   53
+ 68

18)   11
+ 91

19)   77
+ 40

20)   50
+ 63

1)　　23
　　+ 64
　_____

2)　　35
　　+ 26
　_____

3)　　83
　　+ 22
　_____

4)　　60
　　+ 96
　_____

5)　　31
　　+ 41
　_____

6)　　47
　　+ 69
　_____

7)　　48
　　+ 69
　_____

8)　　62
　　+ 16
　_____

9)　　44
　　+ 89
　_____

10)　　35
　　+ 35
　_____

11)　　55
　　+ 50
　_____

12)　　94
　　+ 63
　_____

13)　　61
　　+ 72
　_____

14)　　34
　　+ 89
　_____

15)　　92
　　+ 34
　_____

16)　　82
　　+ 44
　_____

17)　　25
　　+ 78
　_____

18)　　49
　　+ 50
　_____

19)　　79
　　+ 59
　_____

20)　　61
　　+ 16
　_____

1)   86
  + 70

2)   14
  + 96

3)   58
  + 13

4)   54
  + 68

5)   30
  + 22

6)   36
  + 84

7)   38
  + 29

8)   71
  + 47

9)   73
  + 58

10)   74
  + 11

11)   52
  + 91

12)   88
  + 34

13)   91
  + 64

14)   37
  + 33

15)   62
  + 75

16)   80
  + 19

17)   93
  + 50

18)   29
  + 92

19)   13
  + 79

20)   87
  + 86

1)　　75
　　+ 31

2)　　16
　　+ 53

3)　　41
　　+ 27

4)　　89
　　+ 87

5)　　10
　　+ 78

6)　　44
　　+ 93

7)　　70
　　+ 87

8)　　94
　　+ 91

9)　　78
　　+ 10

10)　　91
　　+ 44

11)　　74
　　+ 48

12)　　14
　　+ 84

13)　　76
　　+ 68

14)　　23
　　+ 40

15)　　82
　　+ 33

16)　　21
　　+ 33

17)　　74
　　+ 93

18)　　21
　　+ 84

19)　　54
　　+ 68

20)　　57
　　+ 26

1)   14   2)   15   3)   66   4)   29
    + 60   + 76   + 21   + 76

5)   76   6)   46   7)   52   8)   76
    + 20   + 19   + 75   + 72

9)   59   10)   50   11)   28   12)   69
    + 62   + 70   + 15   + 16

13)   16   14)   44   15)   74   16)   67
    + 40   + 15   + 84   + 33

17)   91   18)   22   19)   97   20)   83
    + 85   + 18   + 22   + 32

1) 76
 + 24
....

2) 13
 + 92
....

3) 52
 + 23
....

4) 27
 + 66
....

5) 63
 + 68
....

6) 74
 + 48
....

7) 78
 + 28
....

8) 84
 + 54
....

9) 73
 + 20
....

10) 76
 + 97
....

11) 11
 + 32
....

12) 22
 + 27
....

13) 17
 + 13
....

14) 52
 + 85
....

15) 41
 + 22
....

16) 27
 + 99
....

17) 50
 + 57
....

18) 55
 + 72
....

19) 70
 + 48
....

20) 18
 + 26
....

1)   71
  + 42

2)   35
  + 51

3)   51
  + 74

4)   97
  + 31

5)   72
  + 22

6)   82
  + 35

7)   12
  + 60

8)   17
  + 38

9)   73
  + 87

10)   45
  + 78

11)   27
  + 89

12)   63
  + 40

13)   86
  + 47

14)   78
  + 77

15)   31
  + 11

16)   70
  + 85

17)   63
  + 68

18)   54
  + 58

19)   46
  + 17

20)   82
  + 17

1) 95 + 30

2) 99 + 72

3) 51 + 96

4) 71 + 43

5) 16 + 58

6) 91 + 65

7) 16 + 38

8) 48 + 62

9) 10 + 54

10) 23 + 86

11) 69 + 18

12) 21 + 33

13) 29 + 57

14) 46 + 57

15) 46 + 73

16) 79 + 51

17) 53 + 78

18) 21 + 21

19) 64 + 27

20) 68 + 30

1) $\begin{array}{r} 60 \\ + 25 \\ \hline \end{array}$
2) $\begin{array}{r} 96 \\ + 42 \\ \hline \end{array}$
3) $\begin{array}{r} 78 \\ + 49 \\ \hline \end{array}$
4) $\begin{array}{r} 23 \\ + 37 \\ \hline \end{array}$

5) $\begin{array}{r} 27 \\ + 37 \\ \hline \end{array}$
6) $\begin{array}{r} 96 \\ + 83 \\ \hline \end{array}$
7) $\begin{array}{r} 85 \\ + 92 \\ \hline \end{array}$
8) $\begin{array}{r} 58 \\ + 36 \\ \hline \end{array}$

9) $\begin{array}{r} 54 \\ + 14 \\ \hline \end{array}$
10) $\begin{array}{r} 27 \\ + 14 \\ \hline \end{array}$
11) $\begin{array}{r} 50 \\ + 35 \\ \hline \end{array}$
12) $\begin{array}{r} 88 \\ + 77 \\ \hline \end{array}$

13) $\begin{array}{r} 92 \\ + 56 \\ \hline \end{array}$
14) $\begin{array}{r} 69 \\ + 75 \\ \hline \end{array}$
15) $\begin{array}{r} 44 \\ + 32 \\ \hline \end{array}$
16) $\begin{array}{r} 12 \\ + 88 \\ \hline \end{array}$

17) $\begin{array}{r} 73 \\ + 74 \\ \hline \end{array}$
18) $\begin{array}{r} 69 \\ + 23 \\ \hline \end{array}$
19) $\begin{array}{r} 47 \\ + 31 \\ \hline \end{array}$
20) $\begin{array}{r} 39 \\ + 66 \\ \hline \end{array}$

1)   79
   + 47
   ----

2)   92
   + 94
   ----

3)   35
   + 19
   ----

4)   20
   + 21
   ----

5)   34
   + 45
   ----

6)   87
   + 33
   ----

7)   74
   + 60
   ----

8)   11
   + 69
   ----

9)   41
   + 58
   ----

10)   15
    + 94
    ----

11)   19
    + 81
    ----

12)   56
    + 36
    ----

13)   88
    + 96
    ----

14)   40
    + 34
    ----

15)   32
    + 43
    ----

16)   86
    + 28
    ----

17)   80
    + 17
    ----

18)   86
    + 65
    ----

19)   87
    + 98
    ----

20)   16
    + 63
    ----

1)   78   2)   88   3)   58   4)   52
   + 85   + 89   + 69   + 67
   ─────   ─────   ─────   ─────

   ....

5)   74   6)   81   7)   52   8)   18
   + 45   + 42   + 52   + 81
   ─────   ─────   ─────   ─────

   ....

9)   27   10)   16   11)   67   12)   84
   + 72   + 78   + 42   + 48
   ─────   ─────   ─────   ─────

   ....

13)   49   14)   14   15)   92   16)   73
   + 19   + 36   + 88   + 31
   ─────   ─────   ─────   ─────

   ....

17)   92   18)   84   19)   47   20)   35
   + 78   + 12   + 74   + 59
   ─────   ─────   ─────   ─────

   ....

1)   65
    + 26
    ....

2)   74
    + 85
    ....

3)   71
    + 60
    ....

4)   49
    + 73
    ....

5)   67
    + 16
    ....

6)   45
    + 53
    ....

7)   46
    + 56
    ....

8)   20
    + 94
    ....

9)   19
    + 81
    ....

10)   46
    + 87
    ....

11)   83
    + 42
    ....

12)   88
    + 61
    ....

13)   18
    + 54
    ....

14)   71
    + 65
    ....

15)   18
    + 48
    ....

16)   11
    + 95
    ....

17)   33
    + 86
    ....

18)   93
    + 52
    ....

19)   97
    + 47
    ....

20)   42
    + 51
    ....

1) $88 + 82$

2) $65 + 29$

3) $15 + 48$

4) $30 + 59$

5) $62 + 66$

6) $97 + 70$

7) $49 + 95$

8) $74 + 32$

9) $37 + 57$

10) $65 + 81$

11) $72 + 68$

12) $48 + 42$

13) $20 + 81$

14) $91 + 70$

15) $32 + 70$

16) $25 + 84$

17) $70 + 26$

18) $62 + 39$

19) $95 + 85$

20) $35 + 57$

SUBTRACTION

SUBTRACTION

1) 22
  - 12
  ....

2) 91
  - 79
  ....

3) 98
  - 62
  ....

4) 84
  - 73
  ....

5) 28
  - 16
  ....

6) 14
  - 13
  ....

7) 54
  - 25
  ....

8) 26
  - 23
  ....

9) 49
  - 31
  ....

10) 97
   - 19
  ....

11) 12
   - 11
  ....

12) 42
   - 40
  ....

13) 79
   - 30
  ....

14) 98
   - 26
  ....

15) 97
   - 21
  ....

16) 91
   - 19
  ....

17) 47
   - 36
  ....

18) 49
   - 41
  ....

19) 17
   - 14
  ....

20) 98
   - 20
  ....

1)   38
  - 34

2)   74
  - 33

3)   48
  - 13

4)   43
  - 34

5)   19
  - 12

6)   12
  - 11

7)   95
  - 87

8)   41
  - 24

9)   87
  - 42

10)   61
  - 20

11)   65
  - 16

12)   53
  - 14

13)   26
  - 22

14)   96
  - 14

15)   29
  - 17

16)   42
  - 17

17)   50
  - 13

18)   81
  - 33

19)   27
  - 22

20)   36
  - 19

1)   20   2)   56   3)   82   4)   19
   - 13   - 43   - 68   - 10

5)   33   6)   22   7)   39   8)   31
   - 14   - 13   - 37   - 26

9)   53   10)   11   11)   28   12)   94
   - 41   - 10   - 16   - 59

13)   80   14)   94   15)   56   16)   30
   - 51   - 58   - 37   - 27

17)   48   18)   74   19)   45   20)   22
   - 13   - 14   - 22   - 10

1)　17
　- 15
　　.............

2)　68
　- 42
　　.............

3)　12
　- 10
　　.............

4)　32
　- 15
　　.............

5)　30
　- 14
　　.............

6)　41
　- 14
　　.............

7)　63
　- 10
　　.............

8)　44
　- 16
　　.............

9)　48
　- 44
　　.............

10)　73
　- 21
　　.............

11)　72
　- 41
　　.............

12)　26
　- 11
　　.............

13)　42
　- 37
　　.............

14)　59
　- 14
　　.............

15)　61
　- 22
　　.............

16)　27
　- 26
　　.............

17)　33
　- 24
　　.............

18)　93
　- 18
　　.............

19)　42
　- 21
　　.............

20)　12
　- 11
　　.............

1)   62
   - 19
   ....

2)   98
   - 48
   ....

3)   88
   - 87
   ....

4)   16
   - 12
   ....

5)   84
   - 16
   ....

6)   88
   - 86
   ....

7)   82
   - 14
   ....

8)   35
   - 34
   ....

9)   98
   - 34
   ....

10)   14
   - 11
   ....

11)   20
   - 13
   ....

12)   26
   - 14
   ....

13)   24
   - 15
   ....

14)   81
   - 35
   ....

15)   63
   - 52
   ....

16)   24
   - 22
   ....

17)   23
   - 12
   ....

18)   97
   - 29
   ....

19)   30
   - 23
   ....

20)   29
   - 25
   ....

1) 27
  - 22
  ⋯⋯⋯⋯

2) 71
  - 12
  ⋯⋯⋯⋯

3) 93
  - 13
  ⋯⋯⋯⋯

4) 83
  - 55
  ⋯⋯⋯⋯

5) 17
  - 11
  ⋯⋯⋯⋯

6) 76
  - 32
  ⋯⋯⋯⋯

7) 15
  - 11
  ⋯⋯⋯⋯

8) 78
  - 24
  ⋯⋯⋯⋯

9) 22
  - 14
  ⋯⋯⋯⋯

10) 27
  - 11
  ⋯⋯⋯⋯

11) 16
  - 10
  ⋯⋯⋯⋯

12) 28
  - 14
  ⋯⋯⋯⋯

13) 73
  - 61
  ⋯⋯⋯⋯

14) 21
  - 16
  ⋯⋯⋯⋯

15) 45
  - 26
  ⋯⋯⋯⋯

16) 45
  - 33
  ⋯⋯⋯⋯

17) 65
  - 39
  ⋯⋯⋯⋯

18) 99
  - 50
  ⋯⋯⋯⋯

19) 13
  - 10
  ⋯⋯⋯⋯

20) 96
  - 54
  ⋯⋯⋯⋯

1)   53
  - 33

2)   70
  - 26

3)   93
  - 43

4)   66
  - 37

5)   47
  - 21

6)   25
  - 11

7)   46
  - 35

8)   42
  - 37

9)   32
  - 31

10)   44
   - 38

11)   51
   - 30

12)   90
   - 73

13)   85
   - 47

14)   37
   - 23

15)   88
   - 38

16)   64
   - 29

17)   76
   - 72

18)   12
   - 10

19)   58
   - 36

20)   39
   - 23

1)   19
   - 11
---

2)   64
   - 13
---

3)   72
   - 61
---

4)   39
   - 24
---

5)   68
   - 22
---

6)   37
   - 29
---

7)   64
   - 59
---

8)   61
   - 41
---

9)   33
   - 22
---

10)   41
    - 19
---

11)   71
    - 14
---

12)   95
    - 70
---

13)   13
    - 11
---

14)   44
    - 11
---

15)   56
    - 40
---

16)   20
    - 19
---

17)   42
    - 13
---

18)   32
    - 14
---

19)   69
    - 46
---

20)   30
    - 10
---

1)　17
− 14

2)　71
− 50

3)　63
− 48

4)　59
− 33

5)　42
− 13

6)　88
− 67

7)　64
− 16

8)　61
− 23

9)　47
− 34

10)　39
− 23

11)　36
− 21

12)　51
− 47

13)　66
− 49

14)　15
− 13

15)　84
− 20

16)　93
− 42

17)　89
− 76

18)　19
− 15

19)　85
− 44

20)　62
− 43

1)   14
    - 11
    ....

2)   90
    - 85
    ....

3)   15
    - 11
    ....

4)   29
    - 24
    ....

5)   24
    - 22
    ....

6)   81
    - 72
    ....

7)   86
    - 59
    ....

8)   29
    - 15
    ....

9)   93
    - 12
    ....

10)   12
    - 11
    ....

11)   75
    - 23
    ....

12)   20
    - 17
    ....

13)   45
    - 20
    ....

14)   15
    - 13
    ....

15)   34
    - 22
    ....

16)   38
    - 15
    ....

17)   64
    - 60
    ....

18)   63
    - 11
    ....

19)   93
    - 20
    ....

20)   44
    - 32
    ....

1)   25
    - 19
    ....

2)   52
    - 38
    ....

3)   57
    - 39
    ....

4)   34
    - 32
    ....

5)   15
    - 11
    ....

6)   40
    - 34
    ....

7)   68
    - 32
    ....

8)   19
    - 15
    ....

9)   56
    - 28
    ....

10)   40
    - 26
    ....

11)   55
    - 26
    ....

12)   61
    - 59
    ....

13)   84
    - 16
    ....

14)   59
    - 11
    ....

15)   98
    - 76
    ....

16)   92
    - 69
    ....

17)   61
    - 42
    ....

18)   53
    - 34
    ....

19)   78
    - 12
    ....

20)   26
    - 22
    ....

1) 16
  - 11

2) 94
  - 36

3) 35
  - 26

4) 31
  - 11

5) 90
  - 53

6) 76
  - 42

7) 29
  - 21

8) 91
  - 63

9) 74
  - 56

10) 99
  - 96

11) 55
  - 23

12) 58
  - 37

13) 48
  - 19

14) 84
  - 51

15) 43
  - 32

16) 59
  - 22

17) 27
  - 23

18) 70
  - 32

19) 91
  - 37

20) 61
  - 27

1)   80 − 58

2)   69 − 23

3)   97 − 53

4)   36 − 22

5)   91 − 55

6)   77 − 36

7)   22 − 18

8)   41 − 39

9)   92 − 59

10) 88 − 56

11) 76 − 46

12) 49 − 40

13) 63 − 23

14) 76 − 32

15) 80 − 73

16) 69 − 41

17) 50 − 31

18) 59 − 56

19) 89 − 22

20) 96 − 27

1) 77
  - 75

2) 71
  - 11

3) 89
  - 27

4) 93
  - 60

5) 20
  - 14

6) 15
  - 14

7) 66
  - 48

8) 14
  - 13

9) 26
  - 24

10) 93
   - 85

11) 18
   - 17

12) 83
   - 68

13) 15
   - 13

14) 13
   - 10

15) 30
   - 16

16) 57
   - 21

17) 50
   - 33

18) 40
   - 21

19) 70
   - 47

20) 78
   - 48

1)   44
   - 37
   ....

2)   76
   - 14
   ....

3)   32
   - 19
   ....

4)   32
   - 20
   ....

5)   45
   - 38
   ....

6)   28
   - 16
   ....

7)   23
   - 17
   ....

8)   23
   - 19
   ....

9)   86
   - 85
   ....

10)   17
    - 12
   ....

11)   92
    - 64
   ....

12)   32
    - 17
   ....

13)   13
    - 12
   ....

14)   63
    - 41
   ....

15)   48
    - 27
   ....

16)   46
    - 22
   ....

17)   25
    - 24
   ....

18)   41
    - 37
   ....

19)   83
    - 17
   ....

20)   60
    - 48
   ....

1)   46
 - 41

2)   87
 - 22

3)   43
 - 17

4)   43
 - 42

5)   69
 - 19

6)   21
 - 14

7)   30
 - 20

8)   87
 - 11

9)   47
 - 26

10) 17
 - 13

11) 23
 - 16

12) 44
 - 41

13) 87
 - 39

14) 37
 - 34

15) 75
 - 25

16) 85
 - 34

17) 80
 - 40

18) 75
 - 43

19) 14
 - 10

20) 82
 - 30

1) $71 - 56$

2) $48 - 20$

3) $23 - 20$

4) $63 - 52$

5) $78 - 35$

6) $96 - 41$

7) $66 - 55$

8) $28 - 18$

9) $28 - 25$

10) $61 - 21$

11) $24 - 10$

12) $20 - 17$

13) $72 - 65$

14) $57 - 29$

15) $47 - 40$

16) $70 - 44$

17) $94 - 12$

18) $63 - 38$

19) $47 - 29$

20) $14 - 12$

1) 44
  - 42

2) 72
  - 34

3) 47
  - 32

4) 29
  - 23

5) 27
  - 14

6) 46
  - 12

7) 26
  - 22

8) 51
  - 38

9) 67
  - 40

10) 58
  - 37

11) 31
  - 28

12) 20
  - 17

13) 71
  - 13

14) 45
  - 42

15) 89
  - 53

16) 49
  - 16

17) 32
  - 29

18) 14
  - 12

19) 75
  - 53

20) 77
  - 59

1)   29
   - 16
   ......

2)   80
   - 55
   ......

3)   80
   - 27
   ......

4)   82
   - 33
   ......

5)   71
   - 63
   ......

6)   96
   - 94
   ......

7)   79
   - 66
   ......

8)   82
   - 62
   ......

9)   53
   - 36
   ......

10) 16
   - 15
   ......

11) 40
   - 25
   ......

12) 71
   - 67
   ......

13) 51
   - 27
   ......

14) 48
   - 30
   ......

15) 91
   - 52
   ......

16) 77
   - 58
   ......

17) 95
   - 42
   ......

18) 56
   - 31
   ......

19) 74
   - 56
   ......

20) 73
   - 33
   ......

1)   82
   - 30

2)   46
   - 16

3)   20
   - 13

4)   13
   - 11

5)   35
   - 19

6)   90
   - 66

7)   84
   - 80

8)   34
   - 18

9)   95
   - 41

10)   23
   - 17

11)   66
   - 48

12)   52
   - 32

13)   77
   - 16

14)   41
   - 35

15)   84
   - 75

16)   58
   - 26

17)   59
   - 46

18)   98
   - 14

19)   31
   - 25

20)   16
   - 15

Emma. School

THANK YOU
FOR SUPPORTING SMALL BUSINESSES LIKE US
IF YOU HAVE SOME TIME, YOU CAN VISIT OUR
STORE ON AMAZON, YOU MAY FIND SOME
BOOKS THAT WILL HELP YOUR CHILD IN
STUDYING

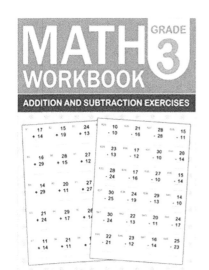
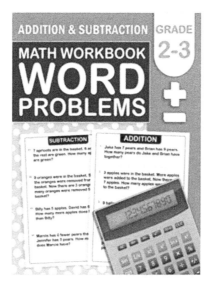

Made in the USA
Columbia, SC
25 June 2022

62226972R00030